HOW TO
BATTLE
DEPRESSION
& SUICIDAL
THOUGHTS

RAY
COMFORT

genesis
PUBLISHING GROUP

How to Battle Depression and Suicidal Thoughts

Published by
Genesis Publishing Group
2002 Skyline Place
Bartlesville, OK 74006
www.genesis-group.net

Edited by Lynn Copeland

Cover, page design, and production by Genesis Group

ISBN 978-1-933591-28-5 (pbk.)

Unless otherwise indicated, Scripture quotations are from the New King James version, © 1979, 1980, 1982 by Thomas Nelson Inc., Publishers, Nashville, TN.

Printed in the United States of America

This story is a work of fiction. All characters and events are the product of the author's imagination. Any resemblance to any person, living or dead, is coincidental.

Depression is a very complex issue, and while it may have a genuine biological basis, many experts believe the vast majority of cases diagnosed as organic depression really aren't.

This content shouldn't be construed as medical advice; please consult your doctor before making any decisions regarding medication.

CONTENTS

CHAPTER ONE

THE GOLDEN GATE BRIDGE

From his bird's eye view, he peered into the foggy bay, as if his solution might be out there just beyond his sight.

Why was he hesitating to take his life? All he had to do was lean forward from the railing and simply freefall into the treacherous depths below, yet he felt as compelled to stay as he did to jump. It wouldn't be painless, but it would be quick, and a lot less painful than this life, he figured.

He felt so hopeless, with no more reason to live. And yet he wanted to.

Oh, how he wanted to.

• • •

I'm not a big fan of crowds. That's why I chose very early on a Tuesday morning, when there are fewer tourists, to walk across the iconic Golden

Gate Bridge. I wanted to get a good sunrise picture for an upcoming publication and the bridge offered an ideal place from which to take the photo. The forecast hadn't mentioned fog, but typical for San Francisco, fog came from nowhere that particular morning. Pea soup. I was deciding whether to turn back or wait for it to clear when I noticed the shadowy figure in the fog about twenty feet from me.

Someone had climbed over the steel railing and was perched precariously on a narrow ledge—and just as precariously on the edge of this life. The ledge was actually about a 30-inch-wide beam, spanning 220 feet above the icy, gray waters of the San Francisco Bay.

As I carefully approached, I saw it was a young man, in his early to mid twenties, with short blondish hair. I was fully aware that a sudden move or the wrong words from me could end in tragedy, so I said a quick prayer for wisdom.

I began by gently asking for his name, telling him mine, and that I'm a Christian and would like to talk with him.

He seemed startled by my approach, but he remained fixed in his spot. "Is that some sort of stage name, for people who need a ray of hope and a little comfort?" he replied wryly.

I assured him that it was my real name and that all I was asking was for him to listen. I'm aware that experts often say to get a suicidal person to talk, but I was afraid talking about his problems may prompt him to jump, and I didn't know how much time he would give me. So, funny as it may sound, I *did* want to give him a ray of hope and some comfort, as quickly as I could. "Even as difficult and painful as your circumstances are right now, you still have tremendous worth. I believe that I can give you some good reasons not to take your life," I said.

"I've already made up my mind. I'm going to jump. You can't tell me anything new that I haven't heard before," he informed me. "And when I jump, what are you going to do? You're going to walk away a failure. Your little speech didn't work. Your little 'God solutions' are irrelevant to the big problems that I have. I've got friends who died and God didn't help them."

"What's your name?" I gently prompted again.

"I'm not giving it to you."

"If you've already made up your mind to jump, you have nothing to lose by listening. Will you give me your word that you won't jump until you hear me out?"

"Why should I give you my word?"

"Okay. You don't know me and you don't know what I'm going to say," I admitted. "Will you let me tell you what happened to my friend's brother?"

"I couldn't care less what happened to your friend's brother. But go ahead," he sighed. "Tell me about your stupid friend's stupid brother."

I wasn't sure how to read his attitude, whether he was still on the verge of jumping or willing to listen, but every minute he continued to talk with me was giving *me* a ray of hope. I continued, "My friend's name is Stuart Scott, and this actually happened in Utah in 2012. A group of masked men with knives took Stan, his younger brother, knocked him out, cut open his chest, and took out his heart. And no one did a thing to stop them."

"Seriously, that's one of the sickest things I've ever heard. There is so much evil in this life!" he exclaimed, his agitation level rising. "That's the kind of thing that gets me so depressed. Everywhere I look I see nothing but horrible things happening. And so how is this supposed to make me change my mind about killing myself?"

"As it stands, you think it was horrible," I quickly told him. "You only think so because you're missing some vital information. What they did wasn't bad. It was good."

"Go ahead, Mr. Wise Guy. Change my mind," he mocked.

"They were surgeons."

"What do you mean?"

"They were heart surgeons who put on their masks, took their scalpels, knocked the man out with anesthesia, cut open his chest, took out his diseased heart that was killing him, and gave him a heart transplant. Those brilliant men saved his life!"

"Oh," he said, meekly.

"*Oh* is right. Just thirty seconds ago you thought that what they did was evil, but now with the missing information you've had a radical change of mind. Just three little words changed your mind from something being despicably evil to being wonderfully good. That little bit of information gave you another perspective, so that you could see the truth."

"Okay... point made. What's that got to do with me standing on the edge of this bridge? It doesn't change my mind about jumping. I'm still going to do it."

"No, the point hasn't yet been made," I said. "The point is, you've made up your mind to take your life, but I'd like to share some information that will give you another perspective. Your life matters, but you think life isn't worth living because you are seeing your situation from your limited point of view. All I'm asking is that you listen to a few words that I believe are going to change everything for you. Will you please hear me out? Just let me run through the reasons that I believe will show you that what you are doing is the wrong thing to do. I don't mean morally wrong. I mean 'wrong' in the sense of it not being in your best interest."

"Okay. I get it. If the information is as radical as you say it is, and it does change my perspective, I give you my word that I won't jump. But I don't think it's going to happen."

"Let's give it a try," I said with a sense of relief. "But I need to know that you won't take offense at anything I say. This is because I'm going to talk about God and other things that may make you feel guilty."

"You make me laugh. I'm on the ledge of the Golden Gate Bridge, about to jump. I have never felt this bad in all my life, and you think you're going to make me feel worse?" He shook his head in disbelief, then added in utter defeat, "I already feel guilty. I feel about as alone as anyone can get. There is no point and no purpose in existing any longer. And you know what? I don't even believe in God; I believe in science and reason. So you have an impossible task. But go ahead. Do your thing."

"Thank you," I replied, greatly encouraged. I knew that *nothing* was impossible . . .

CHAPTER TWO

A WICKED DO-NOTHING GOD

I had been standing on the bridge's walkway, while the young man stood on the ledge, about three feet below, on the other side of the railing. Each time he answered me, it was without looking me in the eye. I wanted to make more of a connection with him, so I asked his permission to sit near him. If I couldn't talk him down off the ledge, just yet, I hoped to at least get him to sit down; that way he'd be less likely to plunge off the bridge while we talked. He agreed. As I sat on the damp sidewalk and looked through a gap in the rail, he was turned slightly so that I could now see most of his face.

"Since you don't believe in God, let's start there," I began. "It's tragic that there's been a recent revival in atheism, so that millions of young people, like you, have been taught to believe there's no evidence for the existence of God. Rather, they see what they think is evidence that God doesn't exist. Just look around at all the starving children, deadly earthquakes, and cancer that kills millions each year."

"Add to that all the evil that goes on in the world, and how can anyone think there is a loving God who takes care of His creation?" he eagerly chimed in. "No; it's more like if there is a God, He's wicked to stand by and do nothing while evil is happening. What sort of father could allow his children to suffer horribly while he stands by and watches? Religion has done nothing to help humanity." He was on a roll now and was becoming more animated. "In fact, its existence has brought evil with it. We would be better off without religion. Think of the thousands of children who have been molested by pedophile priests, and all the simple-minded idiots who give money to rich, slick TV preachers. Religion is responsible for more wars than anything else in history. There is no way you can justify the existence of a loving God in the face of all this!"

"What you're saying is true. These are legitimate arguments," I conceded. It was encouraging to hear him express his views, and these were thoughts that I've heard shared by countless people. "There *is* evil in the world. It's overflowing with evil. But that doesn't deal with the premise of atheism. Atheism claims that there is no God, but you're just saying that if there is a God, He's evil.

"Let's say a man maintains that he built a sky-scraper from the foundation to the hundredth floor. He has the credentials and the experience, and other buildings he can point to, to substantiate the fact that he built the skyscraper. Your argument is that the man is a thief and a liar, and *therefore* the building had no builder. That's an illogical leap. Whether the builder is morally good or bad is irrelevant. Every building has to have a builder. It can't build itself.

"You may be offended at God's seeming inaction when it comes to evil, or at man's evil use of religion," I argued, "but it doesn't negate the fact that we have this intellectual problem of the whole of nature in front of us. Where did it come from? It is scientifically impossible for it to have made itself."

"I thought you were going to offer some evidence of God's existence," he scoffed as he turned toward me. "I want something scientific, something I can hold onto. I don't want this blind faith —believing in some invisible Being in the sky when there is no evidence. Give me evidence and I will listen."

The plentiful gray-and-white seagulls were cawing as they circled directly above us. They were probably just after an early morning feed, but I couldn't help seeing them as circling vultures, smelling death below. It was as though they were goading him with, "Jump. Jump..."

"Okay, I will give you scientific evidence," I began. "Do you believe that a book could make itself? Do you think that it could form its own pages filled with coherent information? There was nothing, then ink fell from nowhere onto paper that came from nowhere, and not only formed itself into sensible sentences, but also into sequential page numbers on each page. More colorful ink formed itself into full-color photos of roses, sunsets, and hummingbirds, then the book designed its own cover. Could a book make itself from nothing?"

"Of course not. That's ridiculous."

"That's right. It is utterly impossible. Are you familiar with DNA?"

"Of course," he said.

"Scientists often refer to DNA as the book of life. It is not only filled with coherent information, but scientists describe it as having letters forming paragraphs and chapters. And this isn't ordinary information; it's *programming* information. Your DNA is so complex that it defies human imagination. From the moment you were conceived, your DNA gave instructions on how to make your eyes, your ears, your skin, your hair, your blood type, your personality…everything about you was written in your DNA from the moment you were conceived."

"Your point?"

"What would you think of the mentality of someone who really believed that a physical book could make itself?" I asked. "To be politically incorrect, he would be crazy. Nobody in his right mind would believe that a book could make itself. So here's my point. What would you think of the intellectual capacity of someone who really believed that DNA made itself? In other words, an atheist. To believe even for a moment that the unspeakably complex programming in DNA made itself makes the person who believes that a book created itself seem sane. Atheism is thoughtless. It is unscientific and senseless. Any rational human being who professes to be an atheist and says that DNA made itself has to be hiding something. They can't be serious."

As I paused to take a breath I wondered whether this was having any impact, but I couldn't see his expression clearly. "So there is your scientific proof for the existence of an intelligent Mind that brought everything into existence. It is outside the realm of possibility for nature to have made itself."

He was quiet for several moments before responding. "Okay, so I guess I'm not an atheist," he answered slowly. "Big deal. It doesn't change anything," he added, a little more defiantly. "It just leaves you with the problem of who this Creator is, why He doesn't say something about Himself, and why He allows evil."

"Good point. That *is* a problem."

CHAPTER THREE

THE PROBLEM OF EVIL

I hadn't planned to be out this long (I suppose neither of us did), and a cool breeze cut through my jacket and brought a chill. My hands were freezing. I wanted to put them in my pockets as we talked, but I didn't want to look even slightly casual. It was miserable, wet, and cold. But the conversation was warming up. "Okay, so now we're back to the character of our Creator. Why would a loving God allow evil?

"Everywhere we look in our world we see evil. It often comes to us as breaking news. A police officer has been shot to death. A white officer has been arrested because he killed an unarmed black youth. A young girl has been viciously raped and left for dead, and the attacker has never been brought to justice. These sorts of things happen every day and are part of human existence. There is evil everywhere."

I continued to reason with him, "But here's the question that needs to be asked: How do we know that evil is evil? What is our point of reference? Is the murder of a cop wrong? If so, why is it wrong? Is rape wrong? How about theft? If so, who says it's wrong? Society? Does rape then become right if society legalizes it? Is murder moral if it is sanctioned by society? If a government under someone like Hitler allows the killing of what they call 'undesirables,' is that morally okay? If society in future generations legalizes pedophilia, does pedophilia become morally acceptable? If not, why not? Societal morality is a slippery slope.

"It is morality that separates man from the beasts," I explained. "Humans have an innate knowledge of right and wrong, and that's why we set up court systems. We have a conscience—a built-in knowledge of what is good and what is evil. Where did that come from? Some of it is obviously shaped by society, but that doesn't explain why every society navigates in some way by the human conscience.

"The existence of evil needs a reference point."

"But that still doesn't deal with your problem of God being evil because of His inaction," the young man argued. "If He was good, He wouldn't let people starve to death, let little kids get cancer, or let young girls be raped and murdered. So you've convinced me that there is a Creator, but I'm convinced that the Creator is evil and I don't want to have anything to do with Him. He even stood by and did nothing while His 'chosen people' were slaughtered by the Nazis. So much for your loving God," he sneered.

"Actually, the problem is bigger than God's inaction with the Holocaust. If you look at the record of the Bible, He also let His people suffer in Egypt and in Babylon. And not only that, if you look at the Christian message, He let His Son be crucified. You may have heard that when Jesus was on the cross He cried out, 'My God, My God, why have You forsaken Me?' Isn't that evidence that God is unloving? But don't be too quick to come to any conclusions. Remember how a little information can give you a completely new perspective and change your mind in seconds."

"Let me ask you a question," he interjected, as another cold breeze blew and sent a chill down my spine. "Do you own a house? Have a well-paying job? A family who loves you?"

"Yes," I nodded. "I do have a wife and kids who love me, I have a good job, and we've had our own home for about twenty years. It's not a mansion, but it keeps the rain out. Why do you ask?"

"Because I have none of those things. When I was fourteen my dad ran off with another woman, abandoning his family and ripping my mom's heart out. I haven't seen him since. After my parents divorced, my mom shacked up with some guy who started out nice, but turned out to be a no-good drunk. He spent all her money, and we lost our house because we couldn't keep up with the payments. I hate my father for doing that to us."

"But that's no reason to want to kill yourself."

"Right. It isn't. My problem started when I got some girl pregnant a couple years ago. We were both at a party one night, half-drunk. I didn't care about her, and so when I found out, I pressured her to have an abortion," he confided. "It was no big deal at the time—just pay out a few hundred bucks and the problem goes away. Someone told me that she ended up cutting her wrists. She didn't die, but she's apparently in some psych ward somewhere. When I heard that, I began to have an overwhelming feeling of guilt. My conscience was eating at me."

He paused, as if weighing whether to continue. Then he went on: "I started using drugs, just recreational at first, to numb the pain. But pretty soon I got addicted, and a few weeks later I got canned at my job for missing too much work. So I started stealing from anyone I could, and then dealing, to keep my habit going. I got caught for possession and had to do three months in jail, followed by twelve weeks of counseling. What a waste of time! Nobody cares."

"What about your family? I'm sure you have people who care about you."

"Sure, until I started lying and stealing from them. My friends say they can't trust me and won't have anything to do with me, and my mom is heartbroken over what I've done with my life. My girlfriend just broke up with me, saying she can't put up with my anger any longer, that I keep taking everything out on her. I don't know why I do that, but I just get so upset at the littlest things. She kicked me out, so now I have nowhere to live. I keep hurting all the people I care about, and I can't take it anymore." He slumped his shoulders and looked deflated, weary of life and its problems.

"I'm sorry you're going through all that. I'm sure that's very painful. But, it's not you they are rejecting," I tried to assure him. "It's the drugs. Do you know what addiction does to you? It steals your dignity. It puts chains around your neck, on your ankles and wrists, and makes you a slave. Then it takes a whip and gives you pain if you don't let it master you. You don't care about eating, or your health, or even hygiene. People become objects to be used and lied to."

"Yeah," he groaned in agreement, "and I've given my mother so much grief she doesn't even want to see me. So I'm alone. Really alone. Seriously, you're the first person I've talked to in depth in a long time…and I don't even know you. And with all that happened, I still can't forget about what I did. I keep asking myself if I killed my own kid. I can't handle that thought. Did I do that?"

"What are you trying to do?" I asked nervously. "Do you want me to say something and have you jump? If you don't mind, I'd rather not talk about that now. I want to ask you something. How long have you been getting bouts of depression?"

"Am I a God near at hand," says the Lord, "and not a God afar off? Can anyone hide himself in secret places, so I shall not see him?" says the Lord; "Do I not fill heaven and earth?" (Jer. 23:23,24)

"The Lord is near to those who have a broken heart, and saves such as have a contrite spirit." (Psa. 34:18)

"The Lord is near to all who call upon Him, to all who call upon Him in truth." (Psa. 145:18)

"Do not be afraid; do not be discouraged, for the Lord your God will be with you wherever you go." (Josh. 1:9)

"For He Himself has said, 'I will never leave you nor forsake you.' So we may boldly say: 'The Lord is my helper; I will not fear. What can man do to me?'" (Heb. 13:5,6)

"Lo, I am with you always, even to the end of the age." (Matt. 28:20)

"Fear not, for I am with you; be not dismayed, for I am your God. I will strengthen you, yes, I will help you, I will uphold you with My righteous right hand." (Isa. 41:10)

"Yea, though I walk through the valley of the shadow of death, I will fear no evil; for You are with me; Your rod and Your staff, they comfort me." (Psa. 23:4)

"Nevertheless I am continually with You; You hold me by my right hand." (Psa. 73:23)

"Who said I'm depressed? Are you just assuming that, because I'm sitting on this ledge?"

His response struck me as slightly humorous, given the circumstances. "Kind of," I said. "You wouldn't want to end your life if you were bursting with joy each morning because you love life. That comes into it. But there is another reason I asked. It's because you said you hate your father. Do you have chronic depression?"

"I suppose," he shrugged.

"When did it start?"

He didn't take long to answer. "When I was about fourteen."

"Around the time your dad left?" I probed.

"Pretty much. But after what he did to my mom, I hated him and was happy to see him go."

"I think your depression is tied directly to your hatred toward your father," I suggested. "Hatred always has baggage. It eats away at the human soul. The Bible says . . ."

Apparently I had struck a nerve and his demeanor suddenly changed. He turned directly toward me with a scowl on his face. "You know what? You're starting to make me mad with your 'The Bible says.' Who do you think you are?" he spat. "You remind me of my father and it's making me feel physically sick. He used to say exactly that, 'The Bible says . . . ,' all the time. He would make me go to church and sit through meaningless drivel. You know what that does to a ten-year-old? I hated it. He was such a hypocrite. He said one thing and did another… 'believe in God,' and then he runs off with a woman at his work. You know what else he did? He bought gifts for her with my mom's money. I really hate him, and your 'The Bible says' is making me want to jump to end it all." Both his voice and his hands were trembling with anger.

"*Please* don't jump," I pleaded. "I'm sorry. I'll be careful with my words. I don't want to stir anything up. If I cause any more problems like that, just tell me."

CHAPTER FOUR

STAY IN THE CHAIR

"Again, I'm sorry. I didn't know about your dad," I said. "I'm trying to do the right thing…"

His reaction wasn't the only thing making me more cautious. The fog was beginning to thin a little, and with the daylight, I was concerned that he might decide to go ahead and jump if someone spotted us. We were making some headway, but I didn't think he was ready to rejoin the land of the living just yet.

"Well, whatever you do, don't try to make me feel guilty about hurting loved ones by my suicide. I know that tactic. Oh, I've thought about that," he said as he leaned back a little, like he was starting to relax. Earlier, I could see the tension in his jaw as though he were grinding his teeth. That suddenly stopped. "I have thought about how my mom will react when she hears the news. Well, don't worry, nobody's going to have to find my dead body hanging in the closet. No one will have to clean my brains off a wall. I've thought it out: what's going to kill me is the impact of the water. It'll be quick and clean. Sure, they'll have a nice funeral; there will be a few tears shed and some people may feel guilty. But they'll get over it.

"I also know that you want to get the suicidal person to talk—I've seen all that on TV. That it's healthy for me to let out my feelings and be distracted from what I'm planning to do. So I'll accommodate you; I'll talk. I'm going to tell you what's going on in my brain. It'll be a great case-study for the experts."

Finally, he was beginning to really open up about his thoughts, and for that I was grateful. I was happy to offer a listening ear.

"You know what's going on in my brain? Fear. Pure terror," he said emphatically, sitting up straight again and looking me in the eye. "It's so powerful it almost takes my breath away. Seriously. I can feel my heart beating in my chest. It's like there are two people living inside my head. No, I'm not schizophrenic and I don't need to see a shrink. One of the voices is cold and calculating. It's pure logic, like Mr. Spock. It tells me that if I want to get out of this mess, if I want to rid myself of this pain and the feeling of hopelessness, this is the logical thing to do. Just jump. It says, 'It will be out of your hands. Gravity will take over and in a second or two you'll hit the water and it will all be over. Simple.'

"But there's another part of me that's like a terrified child. That voice is quietly pleading with me, saying, '*What are you doing?* You can't do this! You value your life. What if right after you jump you suddenly realize you've made the worst mistake of your life? It will be too late.'"

"Keep talking. I'm listening." *And praying,* I thought. I'd often heard that those who consider suicide don't really want to *die*, they just want to end their pain. It was a relief, in a sense, to see that was the case with this young man. His circumstances could be changed and the pains of life dealt with. As long as he was breathing, there was hope.

He continued, "I'm going to be honest with you. Mr. Spock is stronger than the child. I'm afraid he's going to win this battle. Deep down, I want you to talk me out of this—but then what's going to happen after you're gone and his voice comes back even stronger? It will be back to square one. Hopelessness. Helplessness. I can't stand it anymore. Day after day. Even while I'm talking, Spock is pulling me closer to the edge and whispering to me to jump. Please help me!" he pleaded. "Please say something that will help me."

"I can help you. Not because I've been trained in psychology, but because I know exactly how you feel," I openly confessed. We had more in common than he suspected. "I know the feeling of hopelessness. I know the feeling of a fear that is so strong, it takes your breath away. So I ask you to do two things. Number one, and it's the most important

THE GREATEST MISTAKE

"All 29 people who have survived a suicide attempt jumping off San Francisco's Golden Gate Bridge have said they regretted their decision as soon as they jumped." —Dr. Lisa Firestone, PsychAlive

"I just vaulted over, and I realized, at that moment, this is the stupidest thing I could have done. I instantly realized that everything in my life that I'd thought was unfixable was totally fixable—except for having just jumped." —Ken Baldwin

"Instant regret, powerful, overwhelming. As I fell, all I wanted to do was reach back to the rail, but it was gone. I thought, 'What have I just done? I don't want to die. God, please save me.'...I recognized that I made the greatest mistake in my life." —Kevin Hines

Of 515 people who were thwarted from leaping off the Golden Gate, just 6 percent went on to kill themselves. "90 percent of them got past it. They were having an acute temporary crisis, they passed through it and, coming out the other side, they got on with their lives." —Dr. Richard Seiden, "Where Are They Now?"

"I attempted suicide by laying on a set of railroad tracks, and I was run over by 33 freight train cars. I lost both of my legs, but I was still conscious and alive. Thank God!...God had given me a second chance to go to Heaven and spend eternity with Him. I realized my life wasn't mine to take, and I asked Him to forgive me...I am here now with more strength, joy, peace and purpose than I ever imagined." —Kristen Anderson one at this moment, don't listen to Mr. Spock. He's not your friend, he's your enemy. Can you do that?"

"I'll try."

"Second, I want you to trust me. By that I mean, simply believe that my motives are pure in wanting to help you. I don't get paid for this. I am almost as scared as you are, because in a sense your life is in my hands. If I say the wrong thing, or you take something the wrong way, or think that I don't care about you, you could just give up and let go. If you truly trust me, that won't happen. Can I trust you to do that?"

He took a deep breath and exhaled slowly. "I can't promise anything, but I'll do my best to work with you. I don't want to die. But neither do I want to live. So you've got a pretty big task."

"Don't I know it!" Now it was my turn for a deep breath. "But I'm going to give it everything I've got, because, you may not believe it, but I love you and really do care about you, even though I don't know you. Just the fact that you are talking to me is a tremendous encouragement. I have hope, and I hope that I can pass that hope on to you.

"I know that you didn't want to tell me your name. You probably think that I'll call your family. I won't do that. Would you please do me the courtesy of giving it to me? There's an important reason for this," I explained. "I'm going to say things that may seem offensive to you, and to be quite honest, if I can use your name, it will make it easier for me. Please?"

"John," he said quietly, with a half-nod.

"Okay, John," I smiled. "I appreciate that. I'm going to do to you what a dentist does to his patients. He wants to save their teeth, so he's going to go over them one by one looking for decay. If he sees some, he is going to probe it. There is a reason for this. He wants to convince you that your teeth need to be repaired or you're going to lose them. So the temporary pain he causes is for your long-term benefit.

"I'm here because I care about your life. I think you are worth saving. I *know* you are," I stressed. "You are much more than the animal that evolutionists say you are. You're not just a cosmic accident; you're a moral human being made in the image of God. I believe that you have great worth in the sight of your Creator. But like the dentist, the only way I can convince you of that is to cause you some short-term pain. Here is where trust comes in. I want you to trust me for a moment while I probe. Just sit still and let this happen. The end result is worth it."

John mustered as much enthusiasm as you would expect in a dental exam. "Go ahead, Mr. Dentist. I'll stay in the chair."

"I'd like you to do more than stay in the chair. I'd like you to open your mouth wide and let me probe. By that I mean, open your heart to me for a few moments, and be really honest. Can you do that?"

"I've already shared more with you than I have with anyone else in years. So, yeah, no problem."

"Do you think you're a good person?"

"Of course. I've made mistakes, just like everyone else. But, I'm basically good." In a sharp contrast to his previous demeanor, John was suddenly sounding more self-confident.

"How many lies have you told in your whole life? I'm not talking about telling your grandma that her hair is nice, when you think it looks like an abandoned bird's nest. I'm talking about bold-faced lies."

"In my whole life?" He shrugged. "Hundreds."

"What do you call somebody who has told hundreds of lies?"

"A liar."

"You mentioned earlier that you stole things to feed your drug habit. What do you call somebody who steals?" I asked.

"A thief."

"So, what are you?"

"A lying thief," John replied. "But I still think I'm good at heart."

"Have you ever used God's name in vain?"

"All the time."

"Jesus said, 'Whoever looks at a woman to lust for her has already committed adultery with her in his heart.' Have you ever looked at a woman with lust?"

Like almost every male, his reply was emphatic. "Of course!"

CALL ON GOD FOR HELP

"I lift up my eyes to the mountains—where does my help come from? My help comes from the LORD, the Maker of heaven and earth." (Psa. 121:1,2)

"He shall call upon Me, and I will answer him; I will be with him in trouble; I will deliver him and honor him. With long life I will satisfy him, and show him My salvation." (Psa. 91:15,16)

"I sought the Lord, and He heard me, and delivered me from all my fears." (Psa. 34:4)

"In the day when I cried out, You answered me, and made me bold with strength in my soul." (Psa. 138:3)

"From the end of the earth I will cry to You, when my heart is overwhelmed; lead me to the rock that is higher than I." (Psalm 61:2)

"When my soul fainted within me, I remembered the Lord; and my prayer went up to You, into Your holy temple." (Jonah 2:7)

"My soul, wait silently for God alone, for my expectation is from Him. He only is my rock and my salvation; He is my defense; I shall not be moved." (Psa. 62:5,6)

"He heals the brokenhearted and binds up their wounds." (Psa. 147:3)

"Let us therefore come boldly to the throne of grace, that we may obtain mercy and find grace to help in time of need." (Heb. 4:16)

32

"Okay, John, this is where I need you to hold still. Don't flake on me. Please don't get mad, feel hurt, or listen to Mr. Spock. I'm going to tell you the truth about your teeth. Remember, I'm only doing this because I'm seeking your well-being," I said gently. "I'm not judging you; but you have just told me that you are a lying, thieving, blasphemous adulterer at heart. And that's only four of the Ten Commandments, God's moral Law. There are another six we haven't even looked it. So here is the big question: If God judges you by the Ten Commandments on the Day of Judgment, will you be innocent or guilty?"

"I will be guilty as charged," he readily admitted. "If I get judged by that standard."

"Would you go to Heaven or Hell?"

"If I was judged by the Ten Commandments, I would end up in Hell, for sure."

"Does that concern you?"

John shook his head. "No, because I don't believe in Hell."

"That doesn't make any difference. If a judge condemned a guilty man to the electric chair, and the criminal said that he didn't believe in the electric chair, it wouldn't change a thing. They would take him away and execute him, despite his beliefs.

"The Bi…the Scriptures say more about Hell than they do about Heaven. They warn that God will have His day of justice. He is going to punish the evil that so concerned you earlier. Not only murderers and rapists, but also liars and thieves," I added. "You wanted God to do something, and He's going to do it thoroughly, but He is holding off, waiting for you to repent and trust the Savior. He doesn't want you to end up in Hell. So now you see that His inaction against evil actually has a legitimate purpose. It's for your good."

I paused to see how he was taking this. I definitely didn't want him to jump up out of the chair —or off of the bridge. "Please tell me if I'm talking too much, or if you are quietly getting mad at me. I will stop immediately if that's the case. How am I doing, John?"

"Carry on. I can handle the probing."

I continued, "Do you remember how you said that religion has caused more wars than anything else in history? Here are the historical facts. During the twentieth century more people were slaughtered in warfare than in all the preceding nineteen centuries combined. Around 70 million people died in the first two world wars, neither of which were religious. They were political. Most of the wars fought in the twentieth century were similar to the Vietnam and Korean Wars—they were political in nature and had nothing to do with religion. So to say that religion has caused more wars in history than anything else is just not true.

"That being said, religion—meaning the manmade religious system—can't help anybody. It is merely man trying to earn everlasting life by doing religious deeds—fasting, praying, facing Mecca, sitting on hard pews, living a good life, etc. None of these things will bribe God, the Judge of the Universe, to compromise eternal justice. The only thing that can save us from Hell is the mercy of the Judge.

"Can you understand how seeing your own sins changes things?" I pressed John, whose head was now hanging down. "No longer are you an innocent, sinless human being standing in judgment over Almighty God. Now you can see yourself as an evil and justly condemned criminal pointing a holier-than-thou finger at a morally perfect Judge.

"What are you going to do? If you jump from the bridge and die in your sins, your fate is sealed eternally. 'Damned' means just that. There is no way out of Hell. You may feel your life is hopeless now, but that can be changed. However, you won't have a hope in Hell, if you end up there. One second in Hell will make you realize how much you should have valued everything you had on earth. Think about what you used to love and live for," I implored. "A cool drink to satisfy a raging thirst on a hot day. Or your favorite homemade foods, like your mom used to make, when you're really hungry. Or think of a song that brings back such great memories it makes you smile. In Hell there will only be thirst with not a drop to quench it, agonizing pain with no relief, and tormenting fear with no end. It's a place of terrifying punishment, so horrible it defies the imagination, and I desperately don't want you to go there."

My new friend was awfully quiet, and I hoped that he sensed my genuine concern for him, despite these harsh words. "If this sort of talk is beginning to scare you, thank God that it is. Fear is not your enemy, John; in this case, it's your friend. Fear will keep your hand away from a flame and your feet from the edge of a thousand-foot cliff. And if your brain is doing what it should, fear should make you pull back from the very thought of taking your precious life. It was God's incredible gift to you, and you didn't even bother to thank Him. Instead, you ignored Him, and treated Him with contempt. You even spit in His face by using His name as a cuss word. Again, is this getting too heavy for you?"

"No," he answered somberly.

"Right now there is a battle going on in your mind. We have a very real spiritual enemy, who seeks to steal, kill, and destroy us. Satan, the enemy of your soul, wants you to jump. He'd like nothing more than for you to seal your doom in Hell. Who are you going to listen to? The devil, who hates you, or God, who is the lover of your soul?"

I paused to see John's reaction and I silently prayed he was thinking seriously about these things. I continued, "Do you remember how we talked about God's supposed inaction when it came to Jesus on the cross? Here's some information that will change your perspective. Jesus of Nazareth wasn't merely the Son of God. That title actually meant that He was Almighty God in human form.

Now, I'm a little nervous because I want to use that phrase your father used to use. So bear with me. This is what the Bible says: 'God was manifested in the flesh.' 'In the beginning was the Word and the Word was with God and the Word was God...And the Word became flesh and dwelt among us.' The Bible says 'God was in Christ reconciling the world to Himself.' God created for Himself a human body and filled that body as a hand fills a glove. Jesus was the express image of the invisible God. He was born as a human being, lived a morally perfect life, and suffered and died on the cross to take the punishment for the sin of the world. We broke God's Law, the Ten Commandments, and Jesus paid our fine.

"If you're in court and are found guilty, if someone pays your fine, the judge can let you go and still be just. When Jesus was on the cross He cried out, 'It is finished!' In other words, the debt had been paid for our sin. Now God can let us go; He can dismiss our case. He can commute our death sentence and let us live forever, because the fine was paid by another."

"So why did Jesus cry out, 'My God, My God, why have You forsaken Me'—what you mentioned earlier?" John asked.

"Psalm 22, written eight hundred years earlier, explains that when the sin of the world was laid upon Jesus, God, being holy, turned His back on sin. That's why Jesus cried out in torment. Such was His love for you and me.

"Then after Jesus had suffered for our sins, He rose from the dead and defeated our greatest enemy —death itself. The Scriptures say that it was not possible that death could hold Him. Through His resurrection, life overcame death. And now all who repent and trust in Jesus Christ alone as their Savior will receive forgiveness of sins and be granted the gift of everlasting life. Do you think I'm speaking the truth?"

With a slight shrug John answered honestly, "I don't know."

CHAPTER FIVE

THE BAD SIDE
OF PRIDE

I was growing more encouraged that I'd been able to speak with John this long, and that he was patient during the painful probing. As the morning sunlight was breaking through the clouds, I hoped a light was dawning in the darkness of his heart. I also hoped that the lifting fog hadn't alerted the authorities to John and I. I was quietly trusting that there was some sort of divine intervention allowing us to continue.

"What part doesn't make sense?" I gently prompted him.

"Oh, . . . it makes sense," he said hesitantly, still sounding a bit unsure. "You've done a good job. I've never heard it put like that before. My problem is that I have so many questions—about Heaven, my dad, the abortion, and a whole stack of other things."

"Could I ask you to set those questions aside for the moment?" I asked. "They're important, but there is something even more important."

"No problem," John replied.

"We're all made in God's image and have similar basic desires in life. Our common goal in life is to be happy. No human being in his right mind sets out to be unhappy. We have that desire because we have been made like that. Suicide only becomes an option when the fear of life overcomes our intuitive will to live.

"Let me ask you a question, John. It's a personal question and one I want you to think about for a moment before you answer. Are you afraid of dying?"

"There's nothing to think about. I'm not afraid of dying; I never have been," he said without hesitation. "I told you, I don't believe in Hell, so what's there to fear? I'm afraid of the *way* I might die. I don't want some long-drawn-out, painful, cancerous death. I think people should have the right to choose how and when they're going to die. That's why I'm here today. If I could have found a better way to die than jumping, I would have chosen it. The jump scares me, but death itself? No," he shook his head. "I welcome it."

"John, there's something else we all have in common. The Bible, God's instruction book for humanity, tells us that all mankind 'through fear of death have been living all their lives as slaves to constant dread.' It says every human being is a slave to the fear of death. We live in a constant dread of it. I have asked hundreds of people if they are afraid of dying, and I found out something interesting about the answer. People who are humble of heart will admit that they are afraid of dying. They will admit that they think about it all the time and it haunts them. Just like the Bible says.

"But people who are proud won't admit that they have a haunting fear of death," I added, "because it makes them seem vulnerable and weak. So when you tell me that you don't fear death, I hope you don't mind me saying this, John, but I don't believe you. I believe what the Scriptures say about you, because they have proven themselves to be true. The Bible is no ordinary book. It is clearly supernatural in origin, despite what skeptics say about it.

"I have read the Bible every day without fail since April 24, 1972. I have studied it and searched for the supposed mistakes and scientific inaccuracies. They don't exist. They are only in the minds of those who hate the Bible, because it speaks from beginning to end of a God who will hold them accountable."

I paused to give him a chance to respond, but he continued to quietly listen. I knew I was talking a lot, but wanted to share my personal story in case he could relate. "Let me tell you why I am a Christian. At the age of around twenty I became aware of my own fear of death. I wasn't conscious that that was what it was. It was more a sense of heaviness that sat deep within me at the thought that everything I loved—my wife, my mom and dad, everything—was going to be ripped from my hands by this thing called death. This great blackness was swallowing up all of humanity. Nobody spoke about it, but everybody knew it was coming. It didn't matter how rich you were or how politically powerful or famous, death was coming for you. And there's nothing any of us could do about it. All my happiness seemed so futile because it would some day be popped like a bubble by the sharp pin of reality.

"When I read about the millions who suffer from chronic depression, I can identify with them, because that's the feeling that I had before I came to Christ. It was a feeling of helplessness and hope-lessness. There is an elephant in the room waiting to stomp on all of us, and only those who are humble of heart are willing to admit that it scares them.

"Do you think that might be the case with you?"

"Maybe," John half-agreed. Then he sighed. "I take that back. I'm not being honest with you. I *am* afraid of dying," he added quietly. "Terrified. I have been since I was little and it dawned on me that I was going to end up like my grandparents. Dead. I didn't want to admit it to you because I was em-barrassed. I guess that's pride."

"It sure is. We are afraid of what people think of us. I appreciate you admitting it. Most of hu-manity doesn't see anything wrong with pride. But when people have marriage difficulties, you'll often find that pride is what is destroying the relationship. Rather than apologize and say, 'Honey, I was wrong,' pride lifts its ugly head and says, 'I would rather die than apologize.' Pride would rather destroy what was once a good marriage and leave children scarred for life without a father or mother, than back down in humility.

"That sort of pride is a poison, and it is the same pride that holds people back from finding everlasting life. The book of Psalms says, 'The wicked, through the pride of his countenance, will not seek after God.'

"Pride says, 'I would rather go to Hell than apologize to God.' But one second in that terrible place will show that such arrogance is spoken out of ignorance," I continued. "Listen to what Jesus said about that place: 'If your hand or foot causes you to sin, cut it off and cast it from you. It is better for you to enter into life lame or maimed, rather than having two hands or two feet, to be cast into the everlasting fire. And if your eye causes you to sin, pluck it out and cast it from you. It is better for you to enter into life with one eye, rather than having two eyes, to be cast into hell fire.'

"In other words, as much as you value your precious eye, if it causes you to sin, put your finger into your eye socket and gouge it out. And then don't put it down where you can pick it up again. Cast it from you! The imagery is fearful. Think about how you value your eyes. Would you sell one of them for a million dollars?"

"No way," John replied.

"Would you sell both for a hundred million?"

He shook his head.

"Of course you wouldn't. Your eyes give you a window into this beautiful world. If you sold both of your eyes you would be in darkness for the rest of your life. Your eyes are without price. But here Jesus is saying that sin is so serious in God's sight that it would be far better for your eyes to be ripped out than for them to cause you to sin.

"In fact, sin is so serious in the eyes of a holy God that He proclaimed the death sentence upon all those who transgress His Law, and damnation in a terrible place called Hell. What you don't realize, John, is that not only has God seen your lying and stealing, but He has heard every word that has come out of your mouth and seen every thought that has gone through your mind.

"Nothing is hidden from the eyes of Him to whom we must give an account. It was that knowledge that caused me to tremble on the night of my conversion," I confessed. "I didn't realize that God saw my thought-life. He saw my sexual fantasies and what the Bible calls evil imaginations. And every time I sinned, I was storing up His wrath.

"Hey, this is some pretty weighty stuff. Are you still with me, John?"

"Still with you," he mumbled. "And thinking."

CHAPTER SIX

SCARY PICTURE

With the serious topics we were talking about, we both were absorbed in the conversation and oblivious to the growing bustle of traffic passing by. I could feel the bridge shaking as the bigger trucks rumbled past. By now I was convinced that God had led me to the bridge that morning and that He had provided the opportunity to reach out to John.

"I have painted the biblical portrait of God, and it's a scary picture," I acknowledged. "It is filled with wrath and judgment. Nevertheless, it is based on God's revelation of Himself.

"If I told you anything about Him that wasn't in line with Scripture, I would be doing you the ultimate disservice. It would mean that you would have a wrong understanding of your state before God, wouldn't see your need for a Savior, and would end up in Hell. And as I said, John, I am desperate for that not to happen to you.

"But there is something you need to know about this holy and just Creator. He is also loving, compassionate, and rich in mercy. Jesus told three parables to illustrate this. One was about a shepherd who discovered that one of his sheep was missing. So he left ninety-nine sheep and went in search of the one that was lost. When he found it, he lovingly put it on his shoulders and brought it back to safety. That's a picture of the lost sinner."

"Yes, that rings a bell. I remember learning about that story back in Sunday school," John added. "Maybe all that time wasn't a waste..."

"Good to know you recall some of what you heard," I noted. "That's one reason why Jesus told stories—they're memorable. The second parable that Jesus gave was about a woman who lost a coin and searched everywhere for it. When she found it she called her friends and rejoiced that she had found that which was lost. Again, this is a picture of our worth in the sight of God. We are lost, but we are worth finding as far as God is concerned. He rejoices when one sinner comes to repentance."

John's head quietly nodded, either in recognition or agreement, or both. But something else was wonderfully evident. He had turned toward me so that we could look at each other as we spoke, and we were beginning to see eye to eye.

"And finally, Jesus culminated with the story of the lost son. A young man was burning with lust. His hormones kicked in, and like a wild stallion he didn't want to be corralled in his father's household. So he asked his father for his inheritance and then went to a foreign land, away from the eyes of his father, so that he could enjoy the high life. The young man spent all of his money on wild parties and prostitutes. After his money ran out, all of his friends left him, and when a famine came to the land, the only job he could find was feeding pigs in a pigsty.

"As he sat, looking at the pig food, he had a revelation," I continued. "He realized that he was so hungry that he wanted to pick up the filthy corn cobs and eat them. That's when he came to his senses and said, 'Even my father's servants have it better than this. I will go back to my father and say, "I have sinned against heaven and in your sight. Please take me on as a hired servant."' And so he got up out of that filthy pigsty and went back to his father.

"His father, who had been looking for him, saw him at a distance and had compassion on him. He ran to him, fell upon his neck and kissed him. He called for a robe for him and ring for his finger, and he rejoiced, saying, 'My son was once dead and is alive again!'

"The picture of the father watching for his lost son is a picture of God waiting for you to return to Him."

John was looking down, and he put his hand to his chin to rub it thoughtfully. I was pleased to see him slowly nodding again at these stories.

"Yes, I have loved you with an everlasting love; therefore with lovingkindness I have drawn you." (Jer. 31:3)

"What is man, that You should exalt him, that You should set Your heart on him?" (Job 7:17)

"But God demonstrates His own love toward us, in that while we were still sinners, Christ died for us." (Rom. 5:8)

"For God so loved the world that He gave His only begotten Son, that whoever believes in Him should not perish but have everlasting life." (John 3:16)

"In this the love of God was manifested toward us, that God has sent His only begotten Son into the world, that we might live through Him." (1 John 4:9)

"But God, who is rich in mercy, because of His great love with which He loved us, even when we were dead in trespasses, made us alive together with Christ (by grace you have been saved)." (Eph. 2:4,5)

"Oh give thanks to the LORD, for He is good; for His steadfast love endures forever!" (Psa. 118:1)

"I am persuaded that neither death nor life, nor angels nor principalities nor powers, nor things present nor things to come, nor height nor depth, nor any other created thing, shall be able to separate us from the love of God which is in Christ Jesus our Lord." (Rom. 8:38,39)

"Behold what manner of love the Father has bestowed on us, that we should be called children of God!" (1 John 3:1)

"The greatest revelation you will ever have, John, is to realize that your desires have been for filthy pig food. You have wallowed in the filth of sin and loved every minute of it. That's the evilness of our nature: we love the darkness and hate the light. The Bible says that we drink in iniquity like water.

"And where has your sin left you? It has destroyed relationships, cut you off from those you care about, and given you a sense of futility and despair. And it has culminated in thoughts of suicide—to a point of doing yourself the ultimate harm. The pleasure it promised has been outweighed by the pain that it brought. The question is, will you come to your senses?" I gently implored.

"Let me tell you something very personal. Before I was a Christian, I lived for lust. Like every other red-blooded young man, I took great pleasure in looking at girls sexually. But the night of my conversion, when I learned Jesus said that if we looked with lust we committed adultery in our heart, it was like an arrow hit my chest. I knew I was guilty a million times over," I honestly admitted. Yet I was confident this was something John could identify with. "I knew that I had angered God by my sins, but I wasn't sorry. I still wanted to hold onto them. After all, what was left in life if I couldn't look with pleasure at beautiful women? Knowing that I had sinned just made me feel guilty and fearful with no desire to change.

"I want you to listen closely to a story I'm going to tell you. A young boy was once told by his father that a certain vase was priceless. The child was forbidden to touch it or even go near the glass case in which it was displayed. During a trip to the store some time later, the boy noticed an identical-looking vase that cost only five dollars. From then on, not only did the son doubt his father's credibility, but he also lost all reverence for that 'priceless' vase. In fact, one day while his father was out, the boy decided to take a closer look at it. He opened the glass door and carefully handled the family heirloom. It was much lighter than the one in the supermarket, but there was no doubt about it—they were identical!"

I continued, "As he wondered why his father would lie to him about its value, he heard a car pull into the driveway. In his haste to return the vase to the cabinet, he struck it on the glass case and shattered it into a thousand pieces! The child began to tremble with fear. Suddenly he remembered that he had five dollars in his piggy bank and consoled himself with the fact that he could easily replace it. When the father entered the house, the child flippantly called out, 'Dad, I broke that vase thing in the cabinet. It's okay, though. I can get another one at the store with the five dollars I've got in my piggy bank.'

"His father turned pale. He approached his son, placed his hands on the boy's shoulders, looked him in the eyes, and said, 'Son, that was no cheap imitation vase. That was an antique worth twenty-five thousand dollars!'"

John seemed to wince at that. I carried on with my illustration: "The seriousness of what the boy had done suddenly hit him. His mouth went dry. Tears welled in his eyes. He broke down sobbing and fell into his father's arms, saying, 'I'm sorry... I'm so sorry!'

"His father wiped his tears and said, 'Son, there's no way you are going to be able to pay for that vase. It's going to take everything I've got, but I'll pay for a new one myself.' Conflicting emotions gripped the child—horror on one hand that his father would go to such expense, and yet gratitude that he would do such a thing for him despite his deliberate disobedience. Unutterable relief and unspeakable appreciation consoled his grief.

"So, John, let's see how perceptive you are. What produced the boy's sorrow?"

"It came when he saw the seriousness of what he had done," John replied, "revealed in the cost the father would have to pay to make things right."

"That's right," I affirmed. "At the moment, you are aware of the fact that you have broken God's Law into a thousand pieces. But no doubt you're not too concerned, because, like most people, you think that if you face God your good will outweigh your bad—you can make things right yourself. But you can't!

"What did it cost God to justify us—to make things right? The Scriptures tell us that we were not redeemed with silver and gold but with the precious blood of Christ. Our forgiveness was purchased with the unspeakably cruel suffering of Jesus of Nazareth. If you want to catch a glimpse of the cost of our redemption, look to the battered and bruised body of the Son of God as He hung on the cross to take the punishment for the sin of the world. See the blood stream from His wounds. Hear His cry of anguish, 'My God, My God, why have You forsaken Me?' as His soul was made an offering for sin. That was the cost," I said, my voice quaking. I never failed to be gripped with emotion as I considered what Christ had done for me.

"If I gave my life for you, if I stepped in front of a bullet and took it in the chest so that you could live," I added, "it should break your heart. How much more should your heart be broken for your own sins, as you look at what Jesus did for sinners two thousand years ago? The Bible tells us, 'God demonstrates His own love toward us, in that while we were still sinners, Christ died for us.' He did that for us. That's how much value we have to God.

"John, here's something else for you to think about. You are wanting to commit suicide. You want to end life as you know it. Why then not end it all in a different way? When someone is born again, they become a completely new person. The Bible says that old things pass away and all things become new.

"So if you're wanting to end it all, John, here is a way out that will cost you nothing but your pride. Instead of throwing yourself off the Golden Gate Bridge and ending up in Hell, throw yourself into the arms of a faithful Creator, and end up in Heaven."

A car honking as it buzzed past startled us both momentarily, and John looked up. With the water below now growing visible through large holes in the fog, that was definitely safer than looking down. It was then that I saw something that moved me. He closed his eyes tightly and furrowed his brow. With his lips pursed, he let out a long sigh. He probably did it unconsciously, but it revealed his stirred emotions. It was as though he was trembling in his heart. It seemed he was beginning to believe what he was being told, and the implications were breathtaking.

"What do you want—pain and suffering for eternity?" I continued. "By throwing yourself off the bridge you will lose everything, including every pleasure. By throwing yourself into the arms of Almighty God, you will get to keep your precious life, even though you don't value it at the moment. If you do come to Christ today, you will look back in horror at this moment with the thought that you might have chosen Hell over Heaven, merely by letting gravity take over."

John leaned back and closed his eyes again as he listened, his resistance softening. This time there was no furrowed brow or tight lips. Something was happening.

"None of us are worthy of the gift of everlasting life, but in God's eyes we are worth the life of His Son," I emphasized. "What are you going to do in response to such sobering thoughts? Keep your pride, and jump? Or are you willing to humble yourself and apologize to God for your rebellion against His will after He so graciously gave you life?

"John, think about life. Get your mind off the bad things for a moment, and think of the good things...the good things that God gave you. You have eyes. You can see color—the blueness of the sky and the magnificence of a sunrise. You can hear the songs of birds, and the sound of music. Think of all the food you can enjoy. Think of love and laughter. I'm not saying that you should just ignore your pain and be positive. I'm saying more than that...that life is an incredible gift from God to you. It's not something to be trifled with, but looked on with awe. Get up out of the pigsty and run to your Creator. Do that and He will meet you halfway. He will have compassion on you and embrace you as His son."

CHAPTER SEVEN

NO EXCUSE

By now I was sure that there had been divine intervention. As I glanced over my shoulder I could see that drivers were looking in our direction as they sped past. I was eager for us both to get down off the bridge, and wanted to share one more analogy with my friend. I no longer had any interest taking a sunrise picture; there was something of far more value that I was concerned about.

"John, there's one more thought I'd like to leave with you. May I?"

"Sure," he replied, suddenly sounding a little anxious. "You're not going to leave me, are you? I'm beginning to..."

"Of course not! I just want to tell you a true story about a little village in Italy that sits in a deep valley, surrounded by snow-capped mountains. The village, Viganella, is hidden from the sunshine for three freezing months of every year, and those three sunless months are not only cold, they tend to be gloomy and depressing.

"However, the local residents had a bright idea," I explained. "They installed a giant mirror on the mountainside, and it reflected the warmth of sunlight directly into the heart of that dark little town.

"John, I know your life right now seems to be dark, gloomy, and depressing. Life is filled with pain, suffering, and death. But the Bible says that to those who sat in the shadow of death, a light has dawned. Heaven shone its glorious light down to earth in the person of Jesus Christ, the one who said, 'I am the light of the world.'

"Even in the midst of this world's darkness, God has given us light—the light of the glorious gospel. Those who draw near to God can bask in the warmth of His love. If you turn from your sins and trust in Christ, Jesus promises that you will never walk in darkness again. Does that make sense?"

John was silent for a few moments, then asked, "You know what?"

"What?"

"Everything is starting to make sense," he said slowly. "I don't mean about my dad and the other issues that seemed so important. I mean everything makes sense that you've said about God, my sin, and what Jesus did on the cross. I have no excuse for the things I've done. I feel physically sick at what I have become. I even accused Almighty God of being evil! For the first time in my life I understand what happened on that cross. That was the payment for my sin!

"Could you pray for me? Right now!" John pleaded. "I want to pray but I can't. I can't face God. I have never in my life had such an overwhelming desire to kill myself as I do right now. Mr. Spock is screaming in my head for me to jump—seriously! Please pray!" he exclaimed, his voice shaking.

I bowed my head and earnestly prayed, "Father, in the name of Jesus, I stand against every work of darkness. I break every principality and power in John's life, through faith in the name of Jesus. Please help him. I pray that at this very moment, light will flood his soul and that by Your mercy and Your amazing grace, he will pass from death to life. In Jesus' name I pray. Amen."

"Dear God, I...I killed my own child," John began praying, sounding much calmer now. With a refreshing honesty, he opened his heart to his Creator. "I have hated my father. I have used other people for my own selfish needs. I have incessantly lied and stolen, and been filled with sexual fantasies. Help me to get up out of this pigsty. You gave me life, yet I used Your name as a cuss word. I have sinned against You. Please forgive me. Thank You for what You did on the cross. I put my trust in Jesus Christ as my Savior. From this day forward I will live for Him. In His name I pray. Amen."

His eyes, which moments before darted with fear, were now peaceful and resolute. "Would you be kind enough to take my hand and help me up? I want to get away from this place. I have things to do…"

CHAPTER EIGHT

OUT OF THE MOUTHS OF LIONS

The following day as I waited near the counter in my favorite burger restaurant, I was delighted to see a familiar face approaching. "John, I'm so pleased you could make it," I said with a broad smile as I gave him a hug. "Like I mentioned yesterday, I have a few important things I want to share with you." Among other things, I wanted to make sure he was okay, but he was far better than that. For the first time I saw a smile on his face, and his eyes were clear and bright and full of life.

"How could I not come? I love burgers—especially In-N-Out. Yesterday I was miserable and wanted to kill myself and today I'm a Christian being treated to In-N-Out. Gone from hell to heaven in twenty-four hours." He paused to ponder the dual meaning of that thought, and added, "Literally. I can't believe what's happened. Seriously, what you told me was the truth, and I'm excited to hear more."

"Did you want onions? There's such a crowd, I took the liberty of placing your order just before you got here."

"Yes, thanks," John said. "You know what I did yesterday? I went home ... to my mom! I called her first, and when I told her what had happened, that I'd become a Christian, she burst into tears. Well, we both did. I told her I was so sorry for all the pain that I had caused her. When I got off the bus near her apartment, she was standing at the gate looking for me. When she saw me, she ran toward me and hugged me. It was just like that story Jesus told of the father running to his son. Incredible!"

I couldn't stop smiling as John spoke. He hardly took a breath between sentences. "Hold that thought," I said. "Here's your meal. Let's get out of this noise and eat outside. I noticed a table under a tree."

He just smiled slightly, took the food, and carried on speaking with the same wide-eyed intensity.

"And you won't believe this. After dinner, I dug out my old Bible and was reading it. The *Bible!*" John flashed a big grin as he paused, then shook his head as if he couldn't believe it either. "I spent hours reading it and hardly slept a wink last night! I read Psalm 139 and it was so amazing I kept reading it over and over—well, I don't mean I read just *that Psalm* for hours," John chuckled, then continued. "It says that God knows me. From my birth. I've never said one word without Him being aware of it. He created me in my mother's womb, it says.

You know what? The fact that God sees me doesn't freak me out anymore. I don't feel any guilt. Realizing that He sees me makes me feel good, knowing I'm not alone. Am I talking too much?"

"Not at all!" I laughed. "This is making my day. But, you're going to have to hold that thought again. Let's give God thanks for the food."

John was seated, and without saying a word clasped his hands together and once again furrowed his brow. I was about to open my mouth when he beat me to it.

"Dear God, we are so grateful for this day, for the sunrise, for my mom, and for saving me from such a terrible death." His voice cracked slightly. "And thank you for my new friend, for the sound of birds, for music and color. For Jesus and the cross...Oh, and for this food. Amen."

"Amen."

The smell of the fries was suddenly overpowering. I picked one up and placed it on my grateful taste buds.

John didn't miss a beat. He continued, "I had read parts of the Bible a few times when I was in church as a kid but last night it was like it was a different book. I couldn't put it down. I felt like a kid in a candy store."

"Because *you're* different. God gave you a new heart and put His Spirit within you, so you'll find you now have different desires. The way the Bible puts it is that you've been born again and are now a new creature in Christ," I said.

"You ain't kidding. Brand new. It's like a totally new world has opened to me. I can't stop thinking about Jesus, and what He did on the cross—*for me*. And you know what? I've been saying 'Praise the Lord' and meaning it. You know, not in mockery."

I smiled again. "That's wonderful."

"I have so many questions for you. But, I also have one very real fear."

"What's that?"

"I'm afraid that I will lose what I've found. It's a little weird to say this, but I can't describe the feeling of joy. And I have a peace that I never had before."

"You've no worries there," I assured him. "You have God's promise that He will never leave you. Ever. Not even death can separate you from Him."

"Wow, really? That's incredible." John let out a sigh of relief. "Okay, first question—the big one I've been thinking about. What am I going to do if I get depressed? If Mr. Spock starts again, telling me to end it all? How should I deal with thoughts of suicide?"

"Well, let's look at the suicide aspect first. Are you familiar with the story of the Philippian jailer?" I asked.

"I've heard that they have harsh jail sentences for drug users. One of my old friends got two years for less than half an ounce of weed."

"No. Philippian, not the Philipp*ines*. It's a story in the Bible about a jailer who wanted to commit suicide because he thought he messed up at his job."

"Seriously? Just because he messed up?"

"Yes. His employer had a rule that if you blew it, you were put to death. And he thought that he had blown it."

John's eyes sparkled with interest. "Okay. You have me hooked. Give me the details."

"It's in the book of Acts. Two Christians were beaten and then thrown in prison for upsetting the locals."

"What did they do?"

"They cast a demon out of a girl. She had been following them for a long time, yelling out stuff, and one of the Christians, a man named Paul, lost his patience and cast out the demon."

"Do you really believe in that sort of thing? A literal demon?"

The words caught the ear of the young woman sitting behind John. She was sporting devilish tattoos and had brass rings through her nose and in her bottom lip. She turned around slightly and gave a strange look first at John and then at me. I managed a courtesy smile, and answered his question. I could tell that she was straining to hear my answer above the noise of the patio.

"Of course. The Bible has a lot to say on the subject. Anyway, Paul and his friend were beaten and their feet were locked in stocks, and they lay in a cold, dark dungeon, bleeding from their wounds. You know what they did? They sang praises to God."

John looked genuinely mystified. "That's a little weird. Why would they do that?"

"Even in what some may think was a hopelessly depressing situation, they trusted Him. Whatever happens to a Christian happens only by God's permissive will. It may not be His perfect will, but He has permitted it because He can work it out for the Christian's good. More ketchup?"

"Sure, thanks." I sat speechless as I watched him pick up all three of the remaining paper cups of ketchup and smother not more than a dozen fries, and saw them disappear under a sea of red sauce. He continued, "But how on earth could getting beaten up and sitting bloodied and in pain in a cold dungeon work out for their good? Can't see that happening."

I smiled and said, "Would you like to hear what did happen?"

"Of course."

"They're sitting in prison singing hymns…let me read it to you. Hang on—I have a Bible on my phone."

As I reached for my phone, John licked ketchup from his thumb. "Here's another thing that's weird. You know what I like to do? I fry an egg and slip it in-between the patties. An Aussie made me one once. Now I do it all the time," he commented as he bit into his burger.

"I love eggs…ah, here it is. Acts 16:25. Tell you what, take my phone and you read it. Out loud. This burger's got me salivating."

"Okay. Verse 25?"

"Yes. Verses 25 through 31."

John began reading aloud: "'But at midnight Paul and Silas were praying and singing hymns to God, and the prisoners were listening to them. Suddenly there was a great earthquake, so that the foundations of the prison were shaken; and immediately all the doors were opened and everyone's chains were loosed. And the keeper of the prison, awaking from sleep and seeing the prison doors open, supposing the prisoners had fled, drew his sword and was about to kill himself.' So this is the guy who was going to commit suicide. Why would he do that?"

"He was a *Roman* jailer," I explained, between bites. "Under Roman law, if a guard lost his prisoners he was to be put to death for failing his responsibility. Or worse, he would suffer the punishment that was due to his prisoners. It was an effective way to make sure everyone was diligent when guarding prisoners. If his were gone, come sunrise, he would suffer some grizzly death as an example to other jailers who might decide to free condemned prisoners. So he decided to speed up the process."

"That makes sense." John nodded, then he resumed his reading: "'But Paul called with a loud voice, saying, "Do yourself no harm, for we are all here." Then he called for a light, ran in, and fell down trembling before Paul and Silas. And he brought them out and said, "Sirs, what must I do to be saved?" So they said, "Believe on the Lord

THERE IS HOPE

"For I know the thoughts that I think toward you, says the Lord, thoughts of peace and not of evil, to give you a future and a hope." (Jer. 29:11)

"Why are you cast down, O my soul? And why are you disquieted within me? Hope in God, for I shall yet praise Him for the help of His countenance." (Psa. 42:5)

". . . lay hold of the hope set before us. This hope we have as an anchor of the soul, both sure and steadfast . . ." (Heb. 6:18,19)

"Let us hold fast the confession of our hope without wavering, for He who promised is faithful." (Heb. 10:23)

"Be of good courage, and He shall strengthen your heart, all you who hope in the Lord." (Psa. 31:24)

"Now may the God of hope fill you with all joy and peace in believing, that you may abound in hope by the power of the Holy Spirit." (Rom. 15:13)

"Now hope does not disappoint, because the love of God has been poured out in our hearts by the Holy Spirit who was given to us." (Rom. 5:5)

"This I recall to my mind, therefore I have hope. Through the Lord's mercies we are not consumed, because His compassions fail not. They are new every morning; great is Your faithfulness. 'The Lord is my portion,' says my soul, 'Therefore I hope in Him!'" (Lam. 3:21–24)

"Uphold me according to Your word, that I may live; and do not let me be ashamed of my hope." (Psa. 119:116)

Jesus Christ, and you will be saved, you and your household.'" Wow. How cool!"

I set my burger down for the moment. "So when the Philippian jailer was going to kill himself, Paul stopped him. He called out, 'Do yourself no harm, for we are all here!'"

"Kind of like what you did for me," John inserted.

"Right. But think about this. Why did Paul call out? He had a good reason for remaining silent and letting the jailer kill himself. The doors were open and that would have been one less obstacle on the way out. But suicide is never a good choice; it is a *harmful* choice. This was a human being, made in the image of God, and Paul couldn't let the man take his own life."

"So, what does that mean?" John asked as he took a bite and awaited the answer.

"What does what mean?"

Caught with a mouthful, John responded with a muffled, "Made in the image of a God." After he quickly swallowed he added, "You mentioned that yesterday, too."

"It means that God created us in His likeness, with some of His attributes. We are aware of our existence. Consciousness. We can appreciate music and beauty, love and laughter. We have a sense of morality and with it an intuitive passion for justice. Animals don't set up court systems and prosecute other animals that violate some law they have put in place. But humans do. We are unique in creation."

"Wow—I seem to be saying *wow* a lot lately—I've never thought about the difference. I've been told that we are all animals. The whole evolution thing."

"And if you read further," I added, "you will see that the jailer and his whole family came to Christ, and he ended up tending to Paul and Silas's wounds. Then the Romans let them go!"

"So it *did* work out for their good. Amazing."

"Yes. And *there's* the reason no one should ever even think about committing suicide."

A fry on its way to John's mouth paused midair as he asked quizzically, "How do you mean?" Then it found its target.

"Think of what happened. The jailer thought he had good reason to kill himself. The doors were open, so he naturally assumed the prisoners were gone. Life was over. He would never see his beloved family again and would be put to death. It was a hopeless situation, so he may as well do it himself and get it over with.

"But he was wrong—he was not alone. The prisoners were still there! When God is in the equation, what may seem to be a hopeless, depressing, and impossible situation isn't. This is because with God, nothing is impossible." I smiled as I thought of John's comment when we first met: that convincing him life was worth living was "an impossible task." *Truly, nothing is impossible with God.*

"So you're saying that no matter what situation I find myself in, even if there seems to be no way of escape, God can do the impossible," John summarized. "And so if I kill myself, I stop Him from delivering me. I stop the solution."

"Exactly. I'm impressed. Do you know the story of Moses at the Red Sea?"

"You mean the two-by-two…the animals and the ark thing?" John happily continued to work over his burger and fries as I talked.

"No, that was Noah." I couldn't help grinning at this common case of mistaken identity. "Moses was leading the nation of Israel through the wilderness, and they were being chased by an angry enemy—the Egyptian army. They were between a rock and a hard place, trapped at the edge of a sea with no way of escape. But instead of thinking about suicide to get out of an impossible situation, Moses told the people, 'Stand still and see the salvation of God.' Salvation just means deliverance. In other words, even though the situation looked impossible, he trusted God to help. And God did a miracle by opening the sea and providing a way of escape.

"It was a similar situation with a man named Joseph, who found himself in prison wrongly charged with attempted rape. Instead of considering killing himself, he patiently trusted God. And he was delivered. Daniel was tossed into a den of hungry lions, simply for praying to God, and was left overnight. He trusted God and was delivered from their mouths," I concluded, as I hungrily stuffed a few fries in mine.

"Okay. So that's the answer to my question about thoughts of suicide," John summed up. "If they come back, I need to look to God and trust Him."

"Yes, that's the first principle of Christianity. It's foundational," I stressed. "Whatever life throws at you, show that you believe that He will work things out for your good by singing hymns to God, even though you are in pain and chains hold you to your dilemma. Perhaps God will send a miracle your way. You will never know what will happen until you totally trust Him. And singing His praise no matter how bad things may seem is evidence of your trust. Suicide should therefore never be an option. Listen to this wonderful promise in Romans 8:28, and put it in your memory banks so that you never forget it: 'And we know that all things work together for good to those who love God, to those who are the called according to His purpose.' Got it?"

"Got it. *All* things," John repeated. Fries all gone, he popped the last bite of burger in his mouth and crumpled up the wrapper.

"Man, I enjoyed that! You know what I like? The taste of salt that explodes in your mouth when that first hot fry hits the tongue. It's incredible." He shook his head in amazement and added, "This is really strange."

"What's strange?"

"I never used to think like this. Seriously! Fries were just fries. Stick them in the mouth, chew,

YOU CAN TRUST GOD

"But I trust in the LORD. I will rejoice and be glad in Your steadfast love, because You have seen my affliction; You have known the distress of my soul."
(Psa. 31:6,7)

"To you, O LORD, I lift up my soul. O my God, in you I trust." (Psa. 25:1,2)

"Trust in the Lord with all your heart, and lean not on your own understanding; in all your ways acknowledge Him, and He shall direct your paths." (Prov. 3:5,6)

"Who walks in darkness and has no light? Let him trust in the name of the Lord and rely upon his God." (Isa. 50:10)

"You will keep him in perfect peace, whose mind is stayed on You, because he trusts in You." (Isa. 26:3)

"Blessed is the man who trusts in the Lord, and whose hope is the Lord." (Jer. 17:7)

"Whenever I am afraid, I will trust in You." (Psa. 56:3)

"The Lord is my strength and my shield; my heart trusted in Him, and I am helped." (Psa. 28:7)

"In God I have put my trust; I will not be afraid. What can man do to me?" (Psa. 56:11)

"Keep my soul, and deliver me; let me not be ashamed, for I put my trust in You." (Psa. 25:20)

"I will say of the Lord, 'He is my refuge and my fortress; my God, in Him I will trust.'" (Psa. 91:2) swallow. Now I have a whole new appreciation for everything. Did you see the sunrise today? Amazing."

"Yes. It certainly was," I agreed. "Back to Romans 8:28. This doesn't just mean that God will give you light at the end of the tunnel. The promise is that He will work out the situation *for your own good*. He will use your dilemma for your benefit. You may see that in this life, or it may be in eternity. In the book of Hebrews, particularly in chapter 11, you will read about what are often called the heroes of faith, men and women who were put in terrible situations, and yet they trusted God to work things out for good. It would be helpful for you to read that chapter."

"Okay, I will."

CHAPTER NINE

THE SLAP IN THE FACE

"Gentlemen, are you enjoying your meal?" The waiter, dressed in white with a bright red apron and white hat, was a tall, lanky youth.

I looked at his nametag and replied, "It's great. Thanks, Matthias," as I handed him a card. "Did you get one of these? It's six free movies. They are award-winning, seen by millions. The site is on the back of the card: FullyFreeFilms.com."[1]

Matthias smiled from ear to ear, and turned the card over. "Is this for me? No way! Thank you, sir."

As Matthias walked away, John grabbed one of the cards from the small pile that was on the table. "So what are these?"

"They're Christian films," I said, adding that people love being given a card where they can watch six free movies.

---

1 You can find these "Movie Gift Cards" on LivingWaters.com.

"Can I have one? Or a few? I can share them with some friends...if they'll speak to me again."

"Certainly. If you remember, you had asked about what to do when you start to feel depressed."

"Yeah. I would appreciate hearing your thoughts on that," John said.

I polished off my hamburger, ate the last delectable fry, and debated whether to lick my fingers. Then I dove into the next topic of our conversation. "The Bible does have something to say about that, too. Some preachers wrongly promise a bed of roses, when the Christian life can sometimes be a whole stack of thorns. Painful thorns. Did you know that quite a number of biblical figures struggled with depression? Take Jonah for instance."

"Are you telling me that Jonah felt down in the mouth?"

"Very funny," I chuckled.

"Did that really happen?"

"Did what really happen?"

"Did Jonah really get swallowed by a whale?" John asked. "Or is it some sort of Bible lesson about life's circumstances being overwhelming?"

"Well, the Bible does say that a massive fish swallowed Jonah. This is the way I handle strange Bible stories like this," I offered. "I keep in mind that the Scriptures say that God has chosen foolish things to confound the wise, and this certainly is a foolish-sounding story. It is humbling to believe it. It's a stumbling-block for proud people. But Jesus said it literally happened, so I don't doubt it for a second. The premise is that God can do anything. He's not bound by natural laws—that's what 'supernatural' means. Anyway, God used Jonah as a prophet to deliver the people of Nineveh from judgment, and that caused Jonah to go into a big sulk. He actually did get down in the mouth, and hand-in-hand with his pouting came depression—so much so that he sat down and wanted to die. He was actually being childish."

John interjected, "Are you saying that this is what happens with all depression? That people just need to grow up and face life?"

"Definitely not. But it was in this case," I explained, as I took a quick sip. "Jonah was upset that God didn't judge the city, but rather He showed them mercy. If Jonah had a loving heart he would have rejoiced. Instead, his shallow attitude made him jealous and his anger brought on depression. Love fortifies us against such sinful attitudes. A loving person will be glad when good things happen to others. So, John, learn a prophet-able lesson: Don't be shallow in character by letting anger and jealousy into your heart. Anger gives place to the devil, but love keeps the doors shut tight.

"There's a great definition of love from the famous chapter so often quoted at weddings. Well, it used to be, anyway," I added. "One of the modern translations says this (I committed it to memory years ago): 'Love is patient and kind. Love is not jealous or boastful or proud or rude. It does not demand its own way. It is not irritable, and it keeps no record of being wronged. It does not rejoice about injustice but rejoices whenever the truth wins out. Love never gives up, never loses faith, is always hopeful, and endures through every circumstance.' That's from 1 Corinthians 15." I paused to think. "Hang on; that's the resurrection chapter. It's from chapter 13. So much for my memory," I grinned.

"The Bible shows us Jonah's warts. How would you like that?" I asked.

"Like what?"

"How would you like to be featured in the world's most famous book, with all of your personal whining and weaknesses displayed? But that's what we have in the Scriptures. We see the good, the bad, and the ugly (that was great film, by the way). The Bible says that these things were written for our instruction, so that 'we through the patience and comfort of the Scriptures might have hope.' We watch them walk onto landmines, in the hope that we won't follow in their steps."

"And I thought the Bible was just a dry, old history book," John marveled. "Since I became a Christian, it's as though...I don't know how to explain this...it's as though every word is like it's alive. I didn't realize it's so applicable to my life."

I had to smile at that. "Okay, John. Give me a summary of what we have learned from Jonah about what not to do. How can we save ourselves some pain?"

"Well, his angry attitude was childish and unloving. If he was loving, he would have been happy about the good fortune of others."

"That's right," I noted. "Love protects us from sin and its bedfellows, one of which is depression. Have you heard of Job?"

"All I have ever heard is the saying about having the patience of Job. My dad used to mumble that when things didn't go right." This time when John mentioned his father, there was no tone of anger in his voice like there had been the day before.

"Yeah. If anyone was justified in being depressed, it was Job. The Bible says he was a rich man who had everything in life, including being blameless in the eyes of God. He wasn't without sin, but he was better than most. Yet life hit him like a ton of bricks. In one day, he lost all of his wealth and all of his kids were killed in a tragedy. Then he lost his health. Job's suffering was so great that he cursed the day he was born. On top of that, his friends told him that God was punishing him for his sins—which wasn't the case.

"God allowed the storms to pile up on Job for some unknown reason," I continued. "Other than, of course, to teach us how we should react when storms come our way. We are called, like Job, to be patient in tribulation. When we look at the whole picture of his life, though, we see that God not only restored all that he had originally lost, He even gave Job twice as much and blessed him more than before. So it worked out for his good. And that's the consolation that should help us to be patient in tribulation. It really is just a matter of Romans 8:28. Do you remember that verse?"

"Yes. All things work together for good."

"Right. But what's the last part?" I prompted.

"Something about being called."

"'All things work together for good to those who love God, to those who are the called according to His purpose.' The promise is to those who love God. In other words, if you are walking away from the purpose and will of God, it's probably not going to work for your good. I say 'probably' because some Christians may make a wrong business or relationship decision that turns out to be a disaster. They come back to God with a massive mess and, in His kindness, He may work it out for their good. But it sure would have been easier to wait on the Lord for His wisdom before making some life-changing decision. So always commit what you do into God's hands, and if things don't go the way you expect, you can rest in the promise of Romans 8:28. That will help to lift the weight of depression from your shoulders."

John said, nodding, "I'll try to remember that."

"Job wasn't the only one who cursed the day of his birth. So did the prophet Jeremiah, who endured such grief for years that he's known as 'the weeping prophet.' Both Job and Jeremiah wished they'd never been born. Others were more direct and actually prayed to die. In addition to Jonah, the prophet Elijah and Moses both asked God to kill them. It's interesting to note that these men didn't take their own lives by suicide; instead, all three appealed to God to take their lives from them. What do you make of that?"

"Hmm." John thought a moment before replying. "Okay. Tell me if I'm getting the message right. Instead of killing themselves, they knew that their life belonged to God, and as the Giver of life, He was the only one with the right to take it. How's that?"

I felt like a father who had just watched his toddler take his first steps. "Bang on," I said. "Nailed it. I think it's very important to realize that these were real people who suffered from real depression, and they were honest with God in pouring out their hearts. When they felt despair, they looked to Him for help. And we should do the same."

"They are so famous it's easy to lose sight of the fact that they were just like us," John observed.

"Yes. The Scriptures show them experiencing the same trials and difficulties that we do, and in many cases we are even given the solutions. For instance, Moses wanted to die because he couldn't bear the heavy burdens he was carrying alone, so God gave him helpers to lighten his load. The same principle is true for you. If you share your concerns with a friend or family member, it will help lighten your burdens and keep your problems from feeling overwhelming."

I continued, "The prophet Elijah, after he had an especially trying time, was exhausted and de-

"Know that the Lord, He is God; it is He who has made us, and not we ourselves." (Psa. 100:3)

"You have granted me life and favor, and Your care has preserved my spirit." (Job 10:12)

"Thus says the LORD who made you and formed you from the womb, who will help you . . ." (Isa. 44:2)

"Look, every life belongs to Me." (Ezek. 18:4)

"Thus says the LORD, who created you . . . 'I have called you by your name; you are Mine.'" (Isa. 43:1)

"And in Your book were all written the days that were ordained for me, when as yet there was not one of them." (Psa. 139:16)

"Do not be overly wicked, nor be foolish: why should you die before your time?" (Ecc. 7:17)

"Whoever sheds man's blood, by man his blood shall be shed; for in the image of God He made man." (Gen. 9:6)

"You shall not murder." (Exod. 20:13)

"Or do you not know that your body is the temple of the Holy Spirit who is in you, whom you have from God, and you are not your own? For you were bought at a price; therefore glorify God in your body and in your spirit, which are God's." (1 Cor. 6:19,20)

"I shall not die, but live, and declare the works of the Lord." (Psa. 118:17) spondent, and God told him to have some food and water, along with rest. How many times do we neglect the simple care of our bodies? Failing to eat right and get a good night's sleep can wear on our emotional and physical health, and lead to depression. So follow your Creator's advice to keep depression in check."

"Wow, this is all really good stuff!" John exclaimed. "I had no idea all this was in there."

It was so good to see his enthusiasm. Being a small part in a chain of divinely orchestrated events in his life was a huge highlight for me. This life so often doesn't turn out well. Every day people kill themselves, and no one gets to give them another perspective. But it had turned out wonderfully well with John. I loved his hunger for the things of God, and I could hardly wait to share more with him.

I said, "Yeah, the Bible is like that. It's an instruction book for life...and for death. Somebody thought of a great acronym using the word 'Bible': Basic Instructions Before Leaving Earth."

John grinned. "I like that!"

"So do I. There's more. Even King David battled deep depression. Do you know his story?"

"Yes. About Goliath."

"That was a different battle. He had one with a bigger giant, and lost."

"I didn't know that."

"Well, I think you will identify with it," I began. "David was walking on the rooftop of his palace when he spotted one of his neighbors—a beautiful woman named Bathsheba—bathing herself. This giant was lust."

"Okay. I get it."

"Instead of fighting this Goliath, David surrendered to it. He committed adultery with her, and then when she became pregnant with his child, he didn't abort her baby; he aborted her husband. The king had him killed. Then he married Bathsheba, and all was well. Neat and tidy. Except that God saw his sin."

"I guess we didn't cover that one in Sunday school. So what happened?"

I could only read John's lips, and concluded that he had said something about Sunday school. Just to our left, a mother seemed oblivious to the fact that her toddler sounded like the engines of a 777 at full thrust. The child's bag of fries had fallen to the ground, and she was too busy feeding another one of her offspring to be concerned with his problem. After what seemed like an eternity, she took a handful of fries from her own supply and slapped them on a napkin in front of him. Immediate silence. Golden silence. I was pleased, and carried on.

"Well, David's sin weighed heavily on him and led him into a deep depression—not unlike your situation."

"That's true," John acknowledged. "It was my sin that got me into a quicksand of hopelessness. The more I struggled, the deeper I went. Wow… thank God He saved me."

I continued, "As David's conscience was eating away at him, he poured out his great sorrow in several psalms. Listen to his words, here in Psalm 38." I looked it up on my phone and began reading portions:

"'I am troubled, I am bowed down greatly;
I go mourning all the day long.
I am feeble and severely broken;
I groan because of the turmoil of my heart...
For I am ready to fall,
And my sorrow is continually before me...
For I will declare my iniquity;
I will be in anguish over my sin...
Make haste to help me,
O Lord, my salvation!'

"When David eventually confessed his sin and cried out to God for mercy, he got it...because God is rich in mercy. God forgave him and washed away all of his sins. The words of David's prayer are recorded in Psalm 51—it's such a beautiful example of confession and repentance, be sure to read it sometime."

"Psalm 51. Okay, I will," John replied, looking deep in thought. He paused and then added, "Let me ask you: God forgave him? Even for murder?"

"Yes...even for murder."

"Seriously? So are you saying that when God forgave my sins He also forgave the fact that I terminated the life of my own child?"

YOUR GUILT CAN BE REMOVED

"Have mercy upon me, O God, according to Your lov-ingkindness; according to the multitude of Your tender mercies, blot out my transgressions. Wash me thoroughly from my iniquity, and cleanse me from my sin...Wash me, and I shall be whiter than snow."
(Psa. 51:1,2,7)

"If we confess our sins, He is faithful and just to forgive us our sins and to cleanse us from all unrighteousness."
(1 John 1:9)

"For I will be merciful to their unrighteousness, and their sins and their lawless deeds I will remember no more." (Heb. 8:12)

"I, even I, am He who blots out your transgressions for My own sake; and I will not remember your sins."
(Isa. 43:25)

"As far as the east is from the west, so far has He removed our transgressions from us." (Psa. 103:12)

"You will cast all our sins into the depths of the sea."
(Micah 7:19)

"There is therefore now no condemnation to those who are in Christ Jesus, who do not walk according to the flesh, but according to the Spirit." (Rom. 8:1)

"But if we walk in the light as He is in the light, we have fellowship with one another, and the blood of Jesus Christ His Son cleanses us from all sin."
(1 John 1:7)

"Yes," I assured him. "The moment you trust in Christ, you are completely forgiven every single sin."

John clenched his fist and held his bent forefinger to his bottom lip, as tears welled in his eyes. I waited a few seconds for him to get his composure.

"So, John," I asked, "what would you say is the point of David's story? What can we learn about how to avoid sliding into depression?"

"Well, people can become depressed when they're struggling with guilt over unconfessed sin—like I was. So the solution is to cry out to God for mercy —like David did—and they'll find forgiveness."

"That's right. God gave you a conscience for your protection, so make sure you listen to it. Confess any sin as soon as you are aware of it. The Bible says that he who covers his sins will not prosper, but whoever confesses and forsakes them will have mercy."

"Excuse me, sir. Are these Christian movies?" It was Matthias. He was still holding the card.

"Yes, they are," I replied.

"Great! I can't wait to watch them. I'm a Christian."

John seemed mesmerized with the conversation. "I became a Christian yesterday!" he chimed.

"No way!" Matthias reached out and shook John's hand. "Congratulations. That's wonderful. Did you see the Bible verses under your cups?"

John tipped his cup, dribbling water on the table. "Proverbs 3:5. Wow! That's so cool."

Matthias automatically took out his rag and wiped off the table. "Nice to meet you. I'd better get back to work. Thanks again for the movies."

I smiled, turned to John and said, "Nice guy. Okay, back to what we were talking about. The New Testament offers a few more ways to avoid depression. In addition to being beaten and thrown in jail, the apostle Paul endured tremendous hardships—far more than most of us ever will—yet he considered them to be 'light afflictions' compared to the glories that awaited him in Heaven. By keeping the eternal view in mind, he was able to not lose heart."

I continued, "Paul also described how he and the disciples had conflicts and fears, were troubled on every side, and had no rest. Little wonder then that he wrote, 'We were burdened beyond measure, so that we despaired even of life.' But he went on to say this occurred so that 'we should not trust in ourselves but in God who raises the dead.'

"Our option as Christians is to trust in God. So here's another verse for you to commit to memory. It's actually the one that's on your cup. Say it after me: 'Trust in the LORD with all your heart...'

"Trust in the LORD with all your heart...," John repeated.

"And lean not on your own understanding."

"And lean not on your own understanding. Got it."

"That's from the book of Proverbs, which is the cream of the wisdom of Solomon. By the way, did you know there was a point where even the wisest man who ever lived found everything distressing and said he hated life? As Solomon discovered, the only lasting meaning in life is found in trusting God."

"Wow, I didn't know. And he was quite a wise guy, huh?"

"The original." I grinned. "And that brings us to Jesus—our ultimate example. God in the flesh. But because Jesus was also a man, He can sympathize with our pain and weaknesses. The Bible says He was 'a Man of sorrows and acquainted with grief,' and there were times when He was so troubled that He groaned in His spirit. The night before He knew He would be crucified, He said that His soul was 'exceedingly sorrowful, even to death.' Does that sound familiar?"

"Yes, it does," John agreed. "That's about how I felt. That's surprising..."

"Here's an important verse—let me read it to you, from the book of John. When Jesus was praying in the garden that night He said, 'Now My soul is troubled, and what shall I say? "Father, save Me from this hour"? But for this purpose I came to this hour.' Do you know what He was talking about?"

"Of course. Jesus came to earth for the purpose of giving His life as a payment for our sins. *My* sins," John added, smiling.

"That's right. Jesus never considered taking His life, even for a moment. Throwing Himself off a high building, like Satan had tempted Him to—or off a bridge—would have prevented Him from fulfilling the purpose for His life. And the same is true for you. God created you for a purpose and gave you life for a reason. There is meaning to your existence here on earth, and you need to look to God to know what that is.

"What I'm saying is that God could use you to say to this generation, like Paul did, that they are not alone and that they should do themselves no harm," I suggested. "Speaking of God using you, tell me, how would you have handled you?"

He looked puzzled. "What do you mean?"

"How would you have handled coming across someone sitting on the edge of eternity on a ledge of the Golden Gate Bridge?"

John wrinkled his brow. "I don't know."

"Well, what was the turning point in our conversation?"

"The turning point…" He picked up his cup of water, took a sip, and said, "When you first approached me, I was really annoyed. You being there complicated things. I didn't want to have anything to do with you. But there was something in your tone. I think it was a gentleness…and a love. I could feel a genuine concern. The turning point didn't come until I began to understand the cross, but that story of the man having his heart cut out of his chest, by the surgeons, was like a hard slap in my face. It suddenly made me doubt what I was planning to do."

"Everyone who is called by My name, whom I have created for My glory; I have formed him, yes, I have made him … This people I have formed for Myself; they shall declare My praise." (Isa. 43:7,21)

"But you are a chosen generation, a royal priesthood, a holy nation, His own special people, that you may proclaim the praises of Him who called you out of darkness into His marvelous light." (1 Pet. 2:9)

"Jesus Christ, who gave Himself for us, that He might redeem us from every lawless deed and purify for Himself His own special people, zealous for good works." (Titus 2:14)

"For we are His workmanship, created in Christ Jesus for good works, which God prepared beforehand that we should walk in them." (Eph. 2:10)

"And this is eternal life, that they may know You, the only true God, and Jesus Christ whom You have sent." (John 17:3)

"that you may walk worthy of the Lord, fully pleasing Him, being fruitful in every good work and increasing in the knowledge of God." (Col. 1:10)

"'You shall love the Lord your God with all your heart, with all your soul, and with all your mind.' This is the first and great commandment." (Matt. 22:37,38)

"Go into all the world and preach the gospel to every creature." (Mark 16:15)

"So that's all you need. Love and gentleness along with the gospel."

"I can do that. There are others I know who are struggling with depression, and I want to share with them what I've learned. This is the answer to every human problem."

"Well, let's say that if the world obeyed the gospel, if they did what you have done—turned from sin and trusted the Savior—life would certainly be better for the human race." There is a wonderful walk-on-water enthusiasm with a new Christian. I didn't want to dampen John's belief that God can fix this broken world. The only hindrance is humanity. So I chose my words carefully. "Think about it. Experts tell us they don't know the cause of chronic depression that leads to suicide, let alone the cure. The best they can do is try to treat the symptoms: mental illness, guilt, self-hatred, a sense of futility, and the agony of hopelessness.

"After many years of seeing chronic depression and suicide grow into an epidemic, I'm convinced, seriously (as you like to say), that the only answer to this terrible dilemma is the gospel of Jesus Christ. It promises a sound mind, complete release from the burden of guilt, purpose for existence, a reason to live, freedom from the fear of death, and the living hope of eternal life. Hopelessness leaves the moment we are born again.

"So despite the fact that we all have our emotional ups and downs, of all people on earth who shouldn't be depressed to thoughts of suicide, it's us Christians. We know God loves us; He proved that with the cross. He has forgiven all of our sins and granted us everlasting life! Think of that for a moment. Then He promises to work all things out for our good. *All* things.

"However, I'm not saying we won't ever feel down as Christians, or even experience depression at times," I added. "Life is filled with trials, and the evil that we talked about, but in Christ we always have hope."

After a study on the subject of suicide, *The American Journal of Psychiatry* reported:

"Religiously unaffiliated subjects had significantly more lifetime suicide attempts... subjects with no religious affiliation perceived fewer reasons for living, particularly fewer moral objections to suicide."

John leaned forward slightly and put his palms on the now clean table. "Well, then let me ask you another question," he said. "I've had friends who became Christians, and for a while things went well with them. They got off of drugs and alcohol, but then suddenly they went back to their old lives! Seriously, what's with that?"

"They were more than likely something called 'false converts'—the Bible speaks a lot about that. Many people think they become a Christian by praying a prayer or joining a church, instead of what the Bible commands: repent and trust in Christ.

Those friends who 'fell away' did so probably because they came to Christ to have their problems fixed, rather than have their sins forgiven. So they weren't truly born again."

Leaning back on his chair again, he said, "Anyway, the reason I brought it up is that I'm afraid *I'll* fall away!"

It was a legitimate concern for a new Christian. I replied, "As I mentioned, nothing can separate you from God's love. Not even death. The Bible says that He who has begun a good work in you will complete it, and that He is able to keep you from falling and present you faultless before the presence of His glory with exceeding joy. So you can trust that He's not going to let you go.

"It's that same trust that will give you victory over depression. Your faith will give you a joy that will sing hymns in the dungeon. And when the enemy whispers for you to kill yourself, the Scriptures say to submit yourself to God and resist the devil, and he will flee from you. Look to God's Word as your guide, and suicide will no longer be an option."

John didn't say a word. He was too busy hanging on to every one of mine.

"It was God who reached out to you as you sat hopelessly on that ledge. It was He who plucked you from the hands of the enemy, took you out of the darkness and brought you into the glorious light," I continued. "And now He has given you and I the same commission that He gave to the apostle Paul.

He said that Paul was 'to open their eyes, in order to turn them from darkness to light, and from the power of Satan to God, that they may receive forgiveness of sins and an inheritance among those who are sanctified by faith in Me.'

"John, take that light to the millions who sit helplessly on the edge of eternity, in the darkness of the shadow of death.

"May He use you to reach many."

"And your life would be *brighter* than noonday.

Though you were dark, you would be like the *morning*. And you would be secure, because there is *hope*."

JOB 11:17

OFFERING HOPE

In her book, *Hope Prevails: Insights from a Doctor's Personal Journey through Depression*, Christian psychologist Dr. Michelle Bengtson said that every week she saw patients with mental health disorders and depression. She would diagnose the condition and make treatment recommendations. However, with all her expertise, she fell into the dark and deep valley of depression herself.

She said, "My greatest shock came when I tried the same treatment suggestions I typically offered my patients—and they didn't work. I tried medication, I participated in therapy, I ate right and exercised dutifully...for me those things weren't enough. Only when I started to understand what depression does to us spiritually, as well as what it cannot do, and then started cooperating with God did I finally begin to experience the chains of depression falling off."

She concluded, "In the midst of my battle, hope was elusive. I wasn't sure I would survive. Actually, I wasn't sure I wanted to survive. But hope—the belief in a purpose, the belief in something better—can make all the difference. Without hope, what reason do we have to get up in the morning? With hope, we want to move forward, press on, get to the other side, and then share with others what we have learned to offer them hope during their times of trial."

"In my thirty years as a practicing psychotherapist, I've never read a book that suggests more helpful and concrete ways of overcoming depression as *Hope Prevails*." —**Pat Wenger**, MA, LPC, MFT

RESOURCES

For more on this vital topic, please watch a free movie called "EXIT."

From Living Waters, creators of the award-winning TV program *The Way of the Master* and the popular movies "180" and "Evolution vs. God," comes the riveting and hope-inspiring film "EXIT."

According to the World Health Organization, a massive 800,000 people take their lives every year —one death every 40 seconds. For millions who suffer from depression and despair, "EXIT" points to a better way. This compelling movie shines a powerful light in the darkness and offers true hope to those who think they have none. Someone you know may be secretly considering their final exit. Watch "EXIT," and share it with those you love.

See **theEXITmovie.com** to watch "EXIT," get details on a 4-session Video Study, and find other help.

If you are considering suicide, please, call the "Suicide Prevention Lifeline" and talk with someone right now. It's free, confidential, and available 24/7.

800-273-8255, SuicidePreventionLifeline.org

For Non-Christians

If you would like additional information on Christianity, please check out the following helpful resources:

The Evidence Bible. Answers to over 200 questions, thousands of comments, and 130 informative articles will help you better comprehend the Christian faith.

How to Know God Exists. Clear evidences for His existence will convince you that belief in God is reasonable and rational—a matter of fact and not faith.

Why Christianity? (DVD). If you have ever asked what happens after we die, if there is a Heaven, or how good we have to be to go there, this DVD will help you.

If you are a new believer, please read *Save Yourself Some Pain*, written just for you (available free online at Living Waters.com, or as a booklet).

For Christians

Please visit our website and sign up for our free weekly e-newsletter. To learn how to share your faith the way Jesus did, don't miss these helpful resources:

God Has a Wonderful Plan for Your Life: The Myth of the Modern Message (our most important book).

Hell's Best Kept Secret and *True & False Conversion.* Listen to these vital messages free at LivingWaters.com.

For additional resources and information
about Ray Comfort's ministry,
visit **LivingWaters.com**.